Heaven
HELP ME

A Christian's (Light-hearted) Guide to Dying With Grace

By ALLISON PRESUTTI

Heaven Help Me!

A Christian's (Light-hearted) Guide to Dying With Grace

By Allison Presutti

© 2025 InkSpire Press ™

All Rights Reserved

InkSpire
PRESS

Illustrations: InkSpire Press ™

Table of Contents

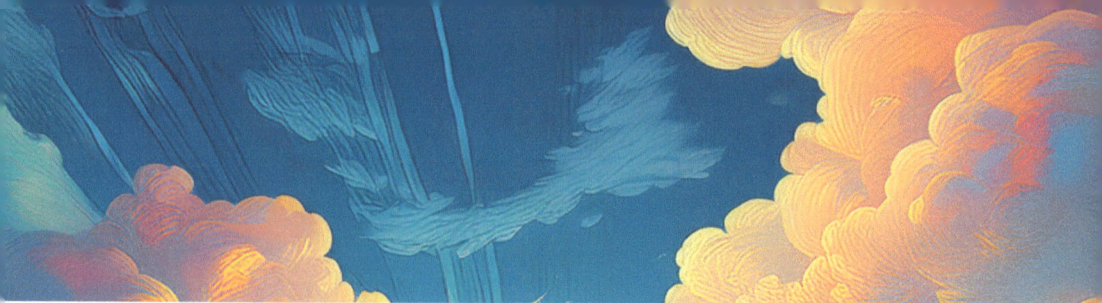

Introduction

Let's face it—talking about death isn't anyone's idea of a fun evening. It's right up there with cleaning out the church basement.

But here's the good news: As Christians, we know that death isn't the end of the story. In fact, it's just the beginning of the really good part. So why not approach it with a little humor, a little grace, and a whole lot of Jesus?

This book is not here to depress you. It's not even here to guilt you into planning your funeral or updating your will (but you should do that). It's here to help you think about the practical and spiritual sides of dying with hope, peace, and yes—some laughs. Because planning for eternity should involve more than just tombstones and tissues. It should include joy. And maybe even a checklist or two.

Whether you're reading this for yourself (because you're a planner with color-coded tabs), or for a loved one who still hasn't updated their voicemail greeting from 2009, this guide is for anyone who wants to face end-of-life decisions with grace and maybe a chuckle or two.

So grab your Bible and your sense of humor. Let's talk about the end of life ... and why, for Christians, it's really just the beginning.

Chapter One

Eternity is handled ...
but the details are on you

Planning your funeral now—before you pass through the pearly gates—is the most loving (and yes, weird) thing you can do.

But let's get one thing straight: You are going to die. That is, unless you're raptured. But in the event you don't fly away, as the song goes, it's best to be prepared.

Now, don't panic. This is just a friendly reminder that, as Hebrews 9:27 so gently puts it, "people are destined to die once, and after that to face judgment." The good news? If you're a believer in Christ, that judgment ends in "no condemnation." (Romans 8:1)

"I'll Fly Away" by Albert E. Brumley, 1929

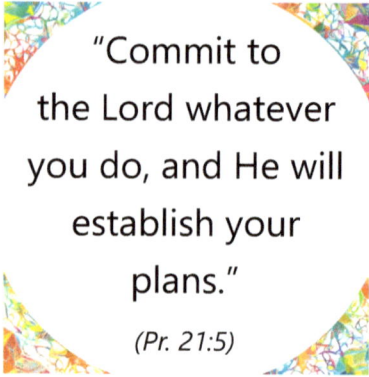

> "Commit to the Lord whatever you do, and He will establish your plans."
>
> *(Pr. 21:5)*

The bad news? Someone still has to pick your casket, choose your favorite hymn, and figure out whether you'd prefer floral arrangements or donations to the local animal rescue.

So, here's the question: Why not do them a favor and plan it out now?

Planning is an act of love

Yes, planning your own funeral may feel like the emotional equivalent of folding fitted sheets—awkward, confusing, and rarely successful—but it's actually one of the most loving things you can do for the people you care about.

By making even a few simple decisions now—songs, scriptures, food—you're removing pressure from the people who love you most. You're giving them permission to grieve without fighting over your favorite casserole dish.

Jesus already took care of the eternal stuff. Your salvation is secure. Your future is glorious. And your mansion has better plumbing than anything on Earth.

But until the trumpet sounds, you've got some details to wrap up. And that, dear reader, starts with grabbing a pen.

Notes: _____

_____

_____

_____

_____

_____

_____

Chapter Two

The ultimate Christian bucket list
(before you kick it to Glory)

❏ Read the Bible cover to cover (even Leviticus ... gulp)

❏ Memorize at least one Psalm—not just Psalm 23

❏ Share your testimony with someone (bonus points if you share with a know-it-all Ivy League student)

❏ Do an all-night prayer vigil... without falling asleep (like Peter did)

❏ Forgive that person (yes, you know the one)

❏ Lead someone to Christ—or plant the seed and let God water it

❏ Take the Lord's Supper without spilling the grape juice

❏ Write a letter to your loved ones to be read after you're gone

❏ Create a "Heaven Hope Box" with verses, letters, or family blessings

❏ Tell your testimony on video or in writing

❏ Raise holy hands during the worship service (you know you want to)

❏ Dance like David (privately or publicly ... up to you)

❏ Go on a mission trip—or support one with a yard sale

❏ Wash someone's feet (and don't be weird about it)

❏ Pack a shoebox for Operation Christmas Child

❏ Watch all the Jesus movies (yes, even the claymation ones)

❏ Do a polar plunge for a church fundraiser (no baptism bonus; that's a separate plunge)

❏ Get baptized (you should have done this already!)

❏ _____

❏ _____

❏ _____

❏ _____

"And the Holy Spirit descended on him in bodily form, like a g~~oose~~ ..."

↳ dove

Luke 3:22

Chapter Three

How to write your obituary before your bitter offspring—oops, your precious children—put their spin on it

Obituary ... or o-bitch-uary? Which will it be? When it comes to your obituary, you've got two choices.

Option A: You write it.

Option B: Your family writes it while half-delirious from grief, bad coffee, and passive-aggressive arguments over who dad (or mom) really loved best.

Also, let's be real, some of our beloved children are, shall we say, more creative than accurate. ("She once saved a drowning possum with nothing but a spatula and a prayer." Sweetie, that was a dream I told you about.)

You can pray your loved ones get it right—or you can make sure they do.

Obituary prompts:

1. What do you want people to remember you for? (Kindness, humor, fierce Scrabble skills?)

   _____

   _____

2. What Scripture sums up your life or gives you comfort? Romans 8:38–39? Psalm 23? Philippians 4:13? (Yes, you have to look them all up.)

   _____

   _____

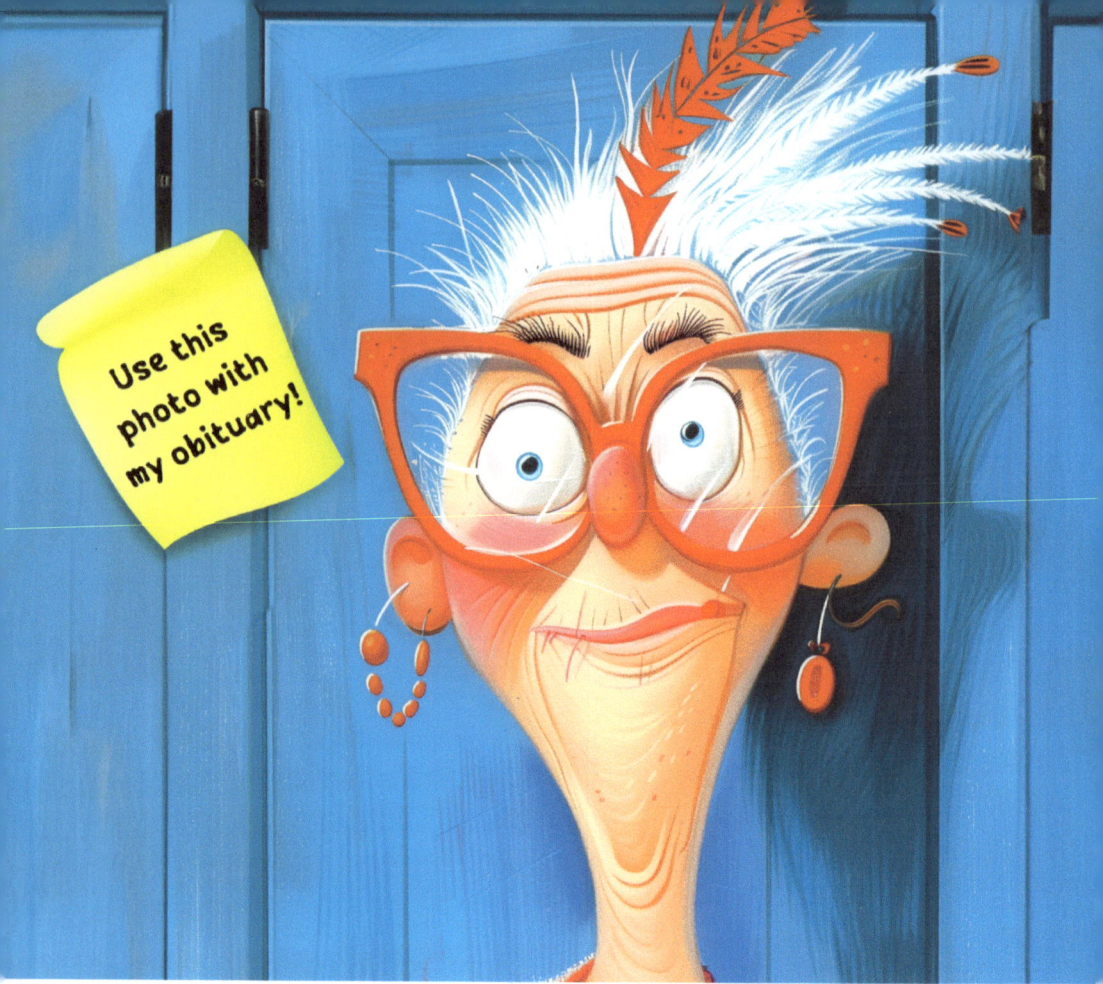

Use this photo with my obituary!

3. Any favorite phrases, hobbies, or quirks? (List two or three, even the silly ones. Especially the silly ones.)

_____

_____

4. What photo do you want to represent your life?

_____

_____

5. What mattered most to you in this life?

_____

_____

6. What brought you the most joy?

_____

_____

7. Signature sayings or quotes:

_____

_____

8. Your weird, wonderful quirks:

_____

_____

9. Hobbies or passions:

_____

_____

10. What people will remember (though you wish they wouldn't):

_____

_____

11. Final blessing or parting words:

_____

_____

Remember: _It's not about perfection. It's about authenticity. When your time comes, you want people to say through the tears, "Yep, that's exactly how Nonna would want to be remembered."_

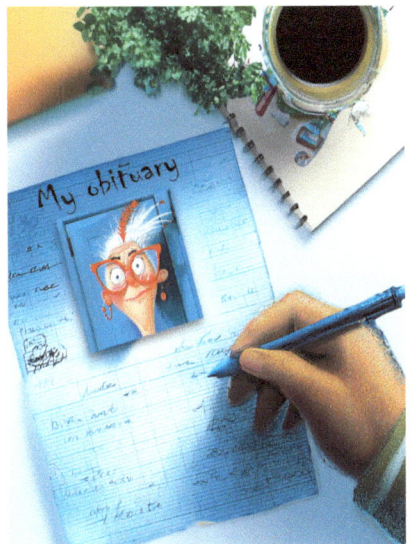

Chapter Four

Jesus take the wheel ... because we don't know who's driving the hearse

Let's be honest: You can trust Jesus with your soul, your salvation, and your sanctification ... but not your transportation. Especially not postmortem.

That's where funeral planning comes in.

Yes, God's got your eternal itinerary covered—but it's up to you to leave instructions for how your earthly vessel gets from point A (the church) to point B (the graveyard) without someone accidentally playing AC/DC on the way.

Note: check local laws; some states do not allow you to wing it on your final ride to Beulah Land.

Do you want a hearse, a horse, or a Ford F-150?

This is your final ride. Make it count.

- **Traditional hearse**—Classic. Black, shiny, and serious. Feels like it should be playing Bach even when parked.

- **Horse-drawn carriage**—Elegant. Especially if you're aiming for "Gone with the Wind" meets "Book of Revelation."

- **Pickup truck with your casket in the back**—Country strong.

- **VW bus or motorcycle procession**—If you spent your life spreading peace and the Gospel on wheels, why stop now?

Who's in the driver's seat?

Here's a little-known fact: When you don't plan your funeral transportation, someone else does—often in a rush, with poor taste in Spotify playlists. Be kind. Give your family a break by:

- Choosing a funeral home ahead of time.

- Picking your vehicle of choice.

- Naming your actual driver. (If legally using transportation other than the funeral home's hearse. Jesus has a better chance of driving a real hearse than one of your relatives.)

- Setting the music vibe. (Silent reverence? Worship music? One last tearful blast of "I Can Only Imagine"?)

Final thought: Don't sweat the transportation. You'll get to the cemetery, one way or another.

Chapter Five

Body or box? Burial, cremation, and other dust-to-dust decisions

Nobody really wants to talk about what happens to your body after you die. That's why people say vague things like "laid to rest" or "passed on" or "gone to be with Jesus" while quietly Googling, "how big an urn will I need to hold all of me, especially since I went off my diet?"

But here's the truth: Your soul may be Heaven-bound, but your earthly remains still need a plan. And unless you want your family to stand awkwardly in a funeral home whispering, "What would Mom have wanted?" It's a holy kindness to sort it out now.

So, let's dive in. Or, you know ... lay down gently.

The classic: Burial

This is the OG of post-mortem options. Jesus was buried. Saints were buried. Most southern grandmas are buried (usually in a plot next to paw-paw sharing a his-and-hers headstone).

Pros:

- Familiar and traditional.

- Allows for a graveside service (and sweet hymns under a tree).

- You get a literal stone with your name on it—kind of like biblical real estate.

- When Jesus returns, He won't have to scavenge the mountains or oceans for every last particle of your ashes. He can do it, of course, because He's ... well, He's God. But why make work for Him? He'll be busy dealing with end-of-the world stuff.

Consider:

- Caskets range from "humble pine" to "this looks like a spaceship."

- Cemetery plots can be expensive (especially if they have a view of Bergdorf Goodman).

- If you're picky about location, pick it now or you might end up next to that noisy cousin in the family section.

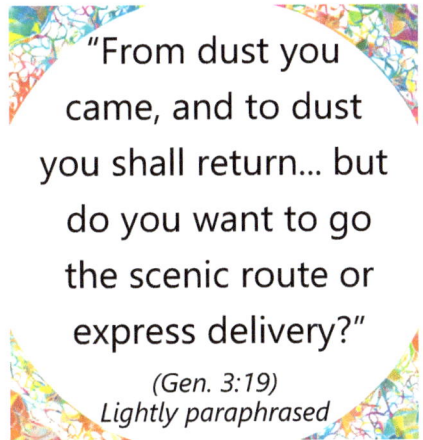

> "From dust you came, and to dust you shall return... but do you want to go the scenic route or express delivery?"
>
> *(Gen. 3:19)*
> *Lightly paraphrased*

Cremation: The hot topic

Cremation has become more accepted among Christians, especially once people realized that the same God who formed Adam from dust can handle ashes just fine because He's ... yep, He's still God.

Pros:

- Budget-friendly (translation: you won't burn a hole in your wallet).

- Portable ashes. Your loved ones can keep you close, or scatter you somewhere meaningful (just check local laws before ending up in someone's rose bush).

- Fewer logistics; no plot required.

Consider:

- Some folks still feel weird about it. Before Christianity spread, cremation was only practiced by unbelievers and commies. (Sometimes one and the same; yes I said it.)

- If you choose cremation, be specific about what to do with your ashes: Urn on the mantle? Garden scatter? Necklace for your niece?

Tibetan Sky Burial: Some people leave a legacy. Others leave leftovers

Alternative options (yes, these are real)

For those wanting to go full eco-friendly (and slightly crunchy-for-Christ), here are some up-and-coming ideas:

*   Natural burial: No embalming, biodegradable casket, back-to-the-earth simplicity. It's humble, holy, Jewish (the founders of our faith, thank you), and compostable.

*   Burial pods: Be buried with a tree seed and become a literal tree. "I am the vine, you are the branches"—see, it works!

- Water cremation: Uses water and heat to return you to dust. Very high-tech and very science-y. May require a fact sheet for Grandma. Never mind; she's being buried next to paw-paw.

- Sky burial: A Tibetan funeral practice where a deceased person's body is placed on a mountaintop to decompose or be consumed by scavenging animals, like vultures. We're putting our foot down on this one. No.

- Donate your body to science: Just make sure your family knows, so they're not surprised when you don't show up at the viewing.

Your faith, your wishes

This is your final resting choice, so let your faith lead. There's no one "right" Christian answer, as long as your heart is focused on Christ, not the container—except for that vulture thing. No again.

Remember: *God isn't worried about your funeral plan. He's preparing your eternal home. But while your loved ones are still here, a little guidance goes a long way.*

Chapter Six

Dressed for the Kingdom—final fashion decisions

You might be clothed in righteousness on the heavenly side, but down here on Earth, someone's still got to pick your outfit for the big day—and it might end up being your sister Tammy who thinks leopard print and polyester are timeless. Do you remember how she looked in middle school? Don't leave this to chance.

Why It matters

Think of your funeral outfit as your final earthly statement. Are you going out in style? In sass? In sweatpants? (Yes, that happens. A lot.) You don't need a stylist, just a sense of what feels you.

Ask yourself:

1. Do I want to be remembered in this?

2. Is this something I would wear if I were attending my own funeral ... as a guest?

3. Will it wrinkle like the Dead Sea Scrolls?

Fashion do's and don'ts of the departed

Do:

- Pick something you loved wearing before you arrived in the Sweet By and By. Fuzzy slippers? Why not. Your body, your choice, right?

- For your funeral, choose clothes that fit well. Let's be honest, you might not be the same shape by then. Gravity still works on Earth, and it's not shy about rearranging things.

- Consider something meaningful—a favorite suit, dress, team jersey, choir robe.

Don't:

- Leave it to chance. That's how you end up in Halloween socks and that shirt that makes you look fat.

- Choose anything with a slogan like "I'd rather be fishing." (Unless, of course, you really would.)

Tips for the fabulous faithful

- Shoes or no shoes? Most people skip them. But if you're picky about your footwear in life, you might want to weigh in.

- Jewelry: A cross necklace or wedding ring can be worn, but make a note of what you want returned and what goes with you to the Celestial Kingdom.

- Hair and makeup: Want to rock your signature red lipstick or that Elvis pompadour one last time? Put it in writing. And maybe include a photo—so the mortician doesn't guess wrong.

Write It Down:

"In the event of my heavenly relocation, please dress me in:"

_____

"And for the love of all that is holy, do not put me in:"

_____

Final Thought: *You might be walking the streets of purest gold, but your body's still taking one final stroll down the aisle. Might as well look good—or at least look like you—doing it. After all, just because you're gone, doesn't mean your style has to be.*

Chapter Seven

Knock, knock, knockin' on Heaven's door: Funeral music that won't offend the angels

There's a holy hush that falls over a funeral when the right music plays ... and a collective grimace when Aunt Carol steps up to the mic with all the confidence of Mariah Carey—but the vocal range of a kazoo.

Let's avoid that.

Why music matters

Funeral music sets the tone. It comforts the grieving, honors your

faith, and helps everyone cry just enough to look emotional without full-blown ugly sobbing. Think of it as the soundtrack to your send-off—one last curated playlist before your celestial upgrade.

The big decision: Live, playlist, or Aunt Carol?

You've got options, friend:

- Live music—Beautiful. Classy. Risky, if Aunt Carol is involved.

- Pre-recorded playlist—Reliable. No pitch problems. Just don't let someone shuffle in "Highway to Hell" by mistake.

- Congregational singing—Sweet and simple, though let's be honest, eighty percent of them don't know the second verse.

Mixing the sacred and sentimental

A good service blends the eternal classics with a touch of your personal flair.

Hymns that slap (spiritually speaking):

- "Amazing Grace" (classic tear-jerker).

- "It Is Well with My Soul" (for drama).

- "How Great Thou Art" (for the crescendo moment).

Contemporary crowd-pleasers:

- MercyMe—"I Can Only Imagine" (obvious, but effective).

- Casting Crowns—"Scars in Heaven."

- Lauren Daigle—"You Say" (for the hip youth pastor vibe).

Optional bonus track:

- That country banjo gospel song you've always loved but never admitted out loud. Yes, that one. We all have one.

Pro tips for a smooth soundtrack

- Make a playlist. Share it. Label it clearly: "Play This When I'm

Dead (Not Kidding)." Include the "Not Kidding."

- Leave written instructions. Don't assume your nephew will know what "that one song from church camp in 1972" means.

- Decide if you want people singing, or just listening while dabbing at their eyes with funeral home tissues.

Write It Down:

- "In lieu of Aunt Carol singing, please play a tasteful recording of
_____."

- "My funeral music should make people cry, then smile, then cry again. Then get saved. In that order."

Final thought: *Worship doesn't stop at the grave—
it just gets louder in the Promised Land. Until then, make your
earthly exit to the music that moved your soul.*

Chapter Eight

The holy ghostwriter: That's you

So you've pre-approved your photo (pomp and pompadour included), and wrangled Aunt Carol's solo into something less ... solo. Now, let's tackle the eulogy—your last mic drop, your grand goodbye, your one last chance to say, "Hey, I was here, and I was fabulous (humbly, and in Christ, of course)."

What is a eulogy, anyway?

Technically, a eulogy is a speech of praise for someone who has passed. Realistically, it's the verbal casserole of a funeral—comforting, sometimes cheesy, and made with love by someone

"Edna suffered from chronic constipation ... but it all worked itself out in the end."

who means well, even if they forget key ingredients (like the correct spelling of your name).

If you don't want your second cousin Todd turning your life into a five-minute awkward confession about the time he kissed you when you were both in pre-school, then—like Paul on a missionary journey—you better chart the course yourself.

Why write your own?

Let's be honest. You know your story best. You know what mattered most, what moments made you laugh till you cried, and what Scripture anchored your soul. You also know which stories should not be told by your prank-loving grandson who thinks it's hilarious to remind everyone about the camping trip with the raccoon.

Writing your own eulogy isn't morbid—it's gracious. It's the final gift of clarity and comfort to your people. Plus, if you write it, you can guarantee someone reads your favorite Bible verse instead of quoting Frozen lyrics.

What to include (and what to skip)

The good stuff:

- Your life's mission in a nutshell. ("She loved Jesus, coffee, and correcting grammar")

- A few highlights. (marriage, family, ministry, victories, baked goods)

- What you learned about God along the way.

- Your favorite Scripture.

- A message of encouragement or faith for those left behind.

The skip-it list:

- Grudges. ("I never liked cousin Brenda and I'm not afraid to say it now.")

- Complicated confessions. (This is not a reverse altar call.)

- Inside jokes only one person will get. (looking at you, Uncle Carl.)

Pro tips for a memorable eulogy

1. Keep it short-ish

People love you. But nobody loves standing for 45 minutes while your eulogy turns into a TED Talk.

2. Make them laugh

Humor heals. If you were funny in life, be funny in death. If you weren't funny, that's okay—just say you tried.

3. Point to Jesus

This is your final pulpit. Even if your life was a mess, let it be a redeemed mess that says, "Look what God can do!" If a lost relative gets saved at your funeral, then you've done your job!

4. Leave a blessing

Imagine your loved ones sitting there, missing you. What do you want them to remember? What comfort can you leave?

Closing thought: *Your eulogy isn't your resume. It's your reflection. It's your last letter to the people who loved you— and a reminder that while you're gone from this world, you're alive in Christ. So, whether it ends with a tear or a chuckle, let your words echo something eternal.*

Chapter Nine

Feeding the flock without starting a food fight

Ah yes, the sacred funeral potluck—a holy tradition almost as vital as the funeral itself. Because nothing says "we loved them" like seventeen casseroles, three kinds of macaroni salad, and a dessert table that could induce a diabetic coma at twenty paces.

This chapter is your guide to coordinating the most glorious post-funeral feast this side of heaven. You may be gone, but your legacy can live on through a well-planned menu—and by making sure your niece Sharon doesn't try to bring her "healthy" tofu loaf again.

Holy guidelines for a heavenly spread

1. **Assign wisely**

   - Don't leave it to chance or you'll end up with five Jell-O molds and zero protein. Delegate categories:

   - Meats & mains (chicken, ham, or "mystery casserole")

   - Sides & salads (potato, macaroni, and that green one with marshmallows)

   - Breads (rolls, cornbread, and gluten-free cardboard for the sensitive folks; you know who they are)

   - Desserts (pies, cakes, and Aunt Deb's famous funeral brownies)

2. **The deviled egg doctrine**

   Yes, they're called deviled eggs. No, it doesn't make them unholy. In fact, they are the universal love language of any church function. If you don't specify who's bringing them, five people will show up with trays—and honestly, that's fine.

3. Label your loaves

It's not a crime to bring store-bought. It is a crime to bring peanut butter bars without warning people that they're peanut butter bars. Allergies are real, cousin Karen.

4. Crockpots are our Heavenly Father's favorite appliance

You can't go wrong with a slow-cooked meal. Just make sure someone plugs them in—and not all into the same power strip like last time. We still haven't recovered from the 2016 "Family Funeral Lunch Blackout."

Avoiding a holy food fight

- **Set the tone:** A sign that says "Love thy neighbor—especially in the buffet line" can go a long way.

- **Monitor the pie count:** If Aunt Phyllis brings her banana cream and doesn't get a slice, there will be a scene.

- **Use name tags:** Not for people—for dishes. No one should have to guess whether that mysterious mush is tuna, chicken, or regret baked into a casserole dish. Save everyone the suspense and use labels.

Include this in your plan:

In your funeral planner or legacy notebook, jot down:

- Preferred potluck coordinator (choose someone responsible, not your cousin who once tried to deep-fry Cool Whip).

- A few of your favorite dishes you'd love to see served.

- Dishes to avoid like the plagues of Egypt (e.g., Sharon's tofu loaf).

- Favorite desserts to request "in lieu of flowers."

- Space for guests to write down their recipes as a keepsake for your family.

Heaven's potluck tip: *Want to be remembered fondly? Pre-write a note to be taped to the dessert table that says, "Eat pie. I insisted." Signed, You.*

or

Consider hiring a caterer. *If the food doesn't suit everyone, you may never hear the end of it. Well ... not you, obviously, but all the "Marthas" in the family who do all the work. You know who you are, and so do all you Marys.*

Chapter Ten

What I'm leaving behind (besides my plants)

Let's face it: you can't take it with you—but you can leave something better than Aunt Emma's collection of Hummel figurines (no judgement; they could be worth a mint). This chapter isn't about stuff; it's about legacy—the heartfelt, the hilarious, and the holy. The things your loved ones will carry long after the casseroles are consumed.

Love letters from the departed

No pressure, but a few well-placed words can mean the world. Write short notes to your spouse, kids, friends, the mailman—whoever mattered to you (yes, even if they always forgot your birthday, but shame on them for that). These aren't essays. Just your voice, your love, your memories, on paper. Want to go extra holy? Include a verse or blessing.

> *"Dear Jake, thanks for mowing my lawn even when I said I could do it myself. I couldn't. May you inherit my mower, and my stubbornness. Love, Mom."*

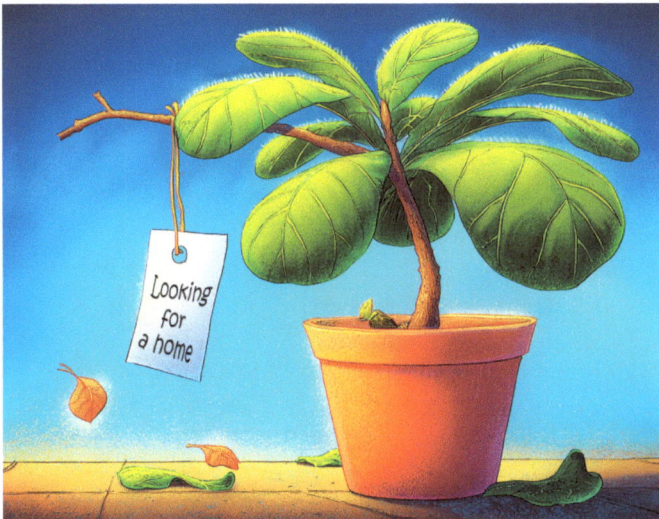

Scriptures to stick with

Of course, they're all good, because they come from the mouth of the Lord, but some are better than, say, Hosea 1:2 ("Go, take to yourself a wife of whoredom and have children of whoredom) when dealing with your end-of-life bequests.

Pick your go-to Bible verses. These can be the ones that anchored you in storms or made you laugh out loud in Leviticus. Your family will cherish knowing which words shaped your walk with God.

Suggestions:

- "Do justice, love mercy, walk humbly." (Micah 6:8)

- "You are fearfully and wonderfully made." (Psalm 139)

- "For I am convinced that neither death nor life ... will be able to separate us from the love of God that is in Christ Jesus our Lord." (Romans 8:38–39)

- "He will wipe every tear from their eyes. There will be no more death or mourning or crying or pain." (Revelation 21:4)

- "The Lord is close to the brokenhearted and saves those who are crushed in spirit." (Psalm 34:18)

- "Jesus wept." (John 11:35). Handy if someone forgets to cry at your funeral.

Things I learned the hard way (so you don't have to)

This is where you pass down pearls of wisdom. Or marbles of mildly useful insight.

- Don't microwave fish in the office.

- Always keep a roll of toilet paper in your car.

- Always keep a Tide To Go pen in your purse.

- Forgive faster than your pride wants to.

- _____

- _____
- _____
- _____

The secret chili recipe

Or your legendary banana pudding. Or that weird-but-delicious dish that only a few diehard family members will go near. Pick one family favorite and write it down. If you're feeling extra dramatic, label it "To Be Opened Only After the Reading of the Will."

About the plants ...

Tell someone who gets sunlight and has good intentions. Or be honest:

"To Whom It May Concern: Please give my fiddle-leaf fig a better life. I tried. I failed. Water it weekly and play it worship music."

Who gets the pets?

This is important, and should be worked out with a loved one before you even think about dying—or before you bark out that first ominous cough.

Final thought: *You might be gone to Sweet Beulah Land, but your words, faith, and fire-breathing chili recipe will live on. Glory be and pass the antacid.*

Chapter Eleven

Final arrangements worksheet

"Dust thou art" ... but please write down how you want your dust handled when you go home to be with the Lord.

1. **My final wishes (pick just one, for obvious reasons)**

   How would you like your remains to be handled?

   ❏ Traditional burial.

   ❏ Cremation.

   ❏ Natural burial (no embalming, biodegradable casket).

   ❏ Donate my body to science.

   ❏ Surprise me (just kidding—pick something, please).

   ❏ _____

2. **Location, location, location**

   Preferred resting place (if applicable):

   _____

   ❏ I already own a plot (location): _____)

   ❏ Please bury me somewhere peaceful.

   ❏ Scatter my ashes at: _____

   ❏ Store me in an urn, but do not, under any circumstances, let me spend eternity sandwiched between the lava lamp and the cursed garden gnome. I will haunt you.

   ❏ Plant me under a tree and name it "Hope" (or something way less cheesy).

   ❏ _____

3. The look (because Heaven and the angels are watching)

Do you have preferences for your earthly appearance at the service?

- ❏ Yes, I'd like to be dressed in: _____
- ❏ I have no preference. Just make me look halfway decent.
- ❏ Who will do the makeup? _____
- ❏ Please include my favorite accessory: _____
- ❏ NO OPEN CASKET. Please, I beg you.
- ❏ I don't want to be viewed at all. You've seen enough of me.

4. Headstone/marker details (if applicable)

- ❏ Yes, I'd like a headstone
- ❏ Please include my full name, dates, and this message:

  _____

Optional:

- ❏ Include a Bible verse: _____
- ❏ Funny quote (optional, but encouraged):

  _____

5. Optional extras (for the righteous overachievers)

- ❏ I'm including a letter to my family to go with these instructions.
- ❏ My passwords and bank account information are located:

  _____

- ❏ Please don't let anyone make a Facebook tribute video without my approval.

❑ I'd like a copy of this worksheet sent to:

Family: _____

Pastor/funeral director: _____

6. Final thoughts

Use this space to say anything else you want your loved ones to know, such as:

> *"I know this is a strange thing to plan, but thank you for honoring my wishes. I hope this makes things a little easier during a hard time. I love you all—and if you don't follow this plan, and if you mess it up, don't be surprised if your toaster starts acting possessed."*

_____

_____

_____

_____

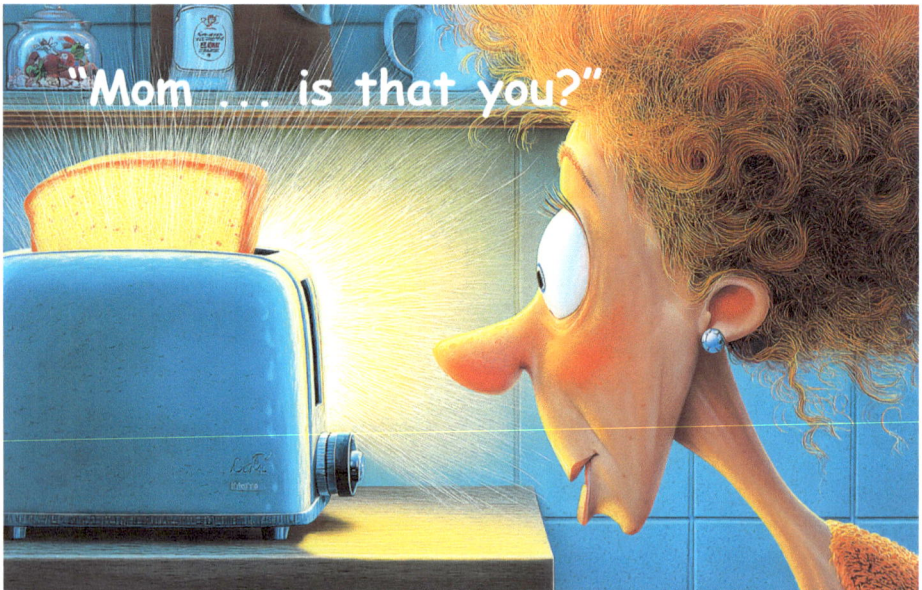

"Mom ... is that you?"

www.ingramcontent.com/pod-product-compliance
Lightning Source LLC
LaVergne TN
LVHW010032070426
835508LV00005B/302